Investing in tax deeds in the United States of America

By

Lisa William

Copyright 2015 @ Lisa_William

No part of this publication should be modified electronically, mechanically or otherwise without the written permission of the copyright owner.

Table of contents

Disclaimer

Introduction

What is a tax deed?

Investing in tax deeds

Tax deed processes

Tax deed states

States procedures

Conclusion

Disclaimer

The following write-up is a guide on how tax deeds are sold across different counties of states of the United States of America. It is not in any way a legal document for the sale or buying of any real estate property. The eBook, if followed will help you in making the best of choices, and it is suitable for newcomers to the real-estate market.

Introduction

You may have saved your money in the bank thinking of what to invest in, and it is making less than 2%. Meanwhile, people are getting richer by the day about 20-60% of their actual money goes into their pockets as profits.

The secret to these is government-backed tax certificates; the certificates are first lien certificates and later on deeds if the taxes are not paid. A lot of states offer deeds directly on properties with delinquent taxes.

In this book, we are treating tax deeds which are issued after a given amount or period accrued on properties of which government taxes are not paid. It is mostly done by auction whereby the local authority publishes the list of properties to be auctioned in the local paper. The bid amount essentially starts with the same amount of back taxes and interests or administrative costs. If you are lucky enough, you buy at the same amount of delinquent taxes, make the necessary payments and voila! The property is yours to rent, occupy or sell as you wish.

But before all this, do your research, know the sale method of each state, the date of the auctions and if possible look for the list of properties of your chosen state and assess their market with similar structures nearby.

What is a tax deed?

A tax deed is a legal document which provides an ownership of a real estate property when the delinquent tax of a property accumulates in which case leading to its foreclosure. The accumulation of the delinquent tax gives the state the authority to sell a property and recover its taxes. For a real estate property, a certain percentage of tax is paid to the government at the end of the certain specific period. The failure to pay the taxes leads to what is known as delinquent taxes (property taxes not paid by the owner) as stated earlier, still, if the owner fails to pay at the delinquent period, the property enters a foreclosure period, and it is auctioned by the government to recover its taxes.

Tax deed sales started a long time ago in the United States of America; the property is auctioned with the minimum starting bid mostly set at the standard amount of fees and back taxes owed. It is issued by the legislating local authority of the place in which the property is situated -- (the country or city-state).

When a tax deed investor buys the property at a foreclosure auction, the ownership of the building is ultimately transferred to him, and the state gets its back taxes. The real owner of the property of which the taxes were incurred has now loose ownership. Although some states of the US allow some period for paperwork processing and sometimes for the delinquent taxpayer to redeem his property if he so wishes, but in which case the one auctioned to will be paid in full with no interest.

In all, the main aim of buying properties at a tax deed auction is to get the property at a price well below market value. The cost will be in most cases, the cost of delinquent taxes plus any additional amount which may accrue due to bidding and some paperwork pennies. Tax deed sale is regulated by state laws and managed by the local authorities.

Investing in tax deeds

Investing in tax deeds in the property boils down to what your goal is in the real estate market or as an investor. They are a sure way of owning a property without the ambiguity of whether or not it will be yours. Thus, you can be flipping real estates for-profit.

About half of the states in America have tax deed opportunities. Foreign investors from anywhere in the worlds have the chance to invest in any country where tax deed is available. The following strategies and procedures should be followed when investing in tax deeds

Contact the person in charge of Tax Deed sales in your area that will be the counties tax collector or treasurer. Ask how the tax deed sales are conducted. Always make sure you have even if minimal a knowledge of what you are getting yourself into.

Study the property very well. Although you may not be able to access it before the sale but make sure you have even if a written knowledge of its description. Is it a standard property that would not require repairs, and what is its market value?

If you are out to make a profit, look for residential homes that can be sold quickly and follow the strategies so as to buy below the standard market value. Although a visit to the property may not be allowed because it is still in the hands of the delinquent tax owner, look at the prospects online or similar properties and their current market value.

There is also another strategy in which a good property, but one which needs renovating is bought. This way, the renovation is done and then sold off at the appropriate market value.

Not only a built house, but you should also look at the possibility of buying lands at tax deed auctions especially the ones situated in developed areas. The vacant land is purchased, developed then sold with a good profit sum.

When a property looks odd to investors and real estate developers, it is often left out. Look for that kind of property and try and buy it at the rate of only the back taxes. You will make a good profit there as well.

Tax deed processes
Choose a suitable location

The majority of tax deed sales are conducted by counties in the United States. Some of the states hold the auction annually, some quarterly. The most important thing is to conduct your research on each of the states and know the one suitable for you. Proximity to your location, timing, and state of the real estate market there should be factored in.

Read and learn about the system

If you are not good at real estates, get a real estate developer to explain the ropes for you. Counties each have their set of rules to the auction. Some counties, for instance, San Diego, offer auctions by item number and re-offer properties without bids at the end again. They open the bids normally with the amount of the delinquent tax and mostly require payment immediately when a bid is won. Try and learn the payment methods for your chosen county.

Obtain the published list of properties

Try and secure the list of all the properties before the auction date. The authority usually publishes the list on their website or request by email. Knowing the physical address will help you in knowing what you are buying.

Conduct your research on the properties

Go for properties with profit potentials. This can be done by looking at similar properties within the same area and knowing the standard market value and the starting bid value for each property. Although these may seem too cumbersome, they will help you make the best of choices. Their market value can be known by checking the local tax authority office. And again look at their size, age proximity to essential social amenities.

Avoid lien properties

Be careful so as not to buy properties with other liens on them. Check on liens which may include some unpaid county fines or other tax liens. Having a lien on a property will raise the price with a corresponding decrease in profit for the investor.

Be present at the Auction

Although some auctions are carried out online, you must be present at those requiring your physical appearance before you can place a bid. Check to confirm you have the requirements for payments because some require immediate while some counties allow some time for payment.

Plan foremost how to make profit

When you win a bid and make all the required payments, the property is now yours. Then you will have to plan your next course of action. Are you staying inside (in the case of a house), selling or renting it out? For quick cash, selling is the best option, but for a steady income over a period, you may want to try renting it out.

Check for map descriptions and bounds legal descriptions

The division and subdivision maps can be found in the clerk's office; they provide the block number, subdivision name, meters and lot number. Other descriptions such as the section, range, and township can be found in the property appraiser's office.

Tax deed states

- Alaska
- Arkansas
- California
- Connecticut
- Delaware
- Florida
- Idaho
- Kansas
- Maine
- Michigan
- Nevada
- New Mexico
- New York
- North Carolina
- Ohio
- Oklahoma
- Oregon
- Pennsylvania
- Tennessee
- Utah
- Washington
- Wisconsin
- Indiana
- Minnesota

States procedures
Alaska

Alaska is a tax deed state, tax lien certificates on delinquent properties are issued annually by the tax collector to the county for filing. After a year of releasing the lien, the property may then be sold when the owner didn't pay the delinquents and the penalties or fees. Boroughs handle the tax deed sales and usually, auctions carried out as sealed bid method to conduct sales or as premium bids.

The lists of available properties to be auctioned are published in the local newspaper before the sale, and up to the auction day, the owner may redeem the property by paying the taxes and some penalties fees if there is. Different methods are used for the auctions in this state; you will have to contact the boroughs to know the method used. They usually issue a number which will be used when bidding.

As mentioned above, the state of Alaska uses two standard methods of buying tax foreclosure which is the sealed bid and the premium bid. The sealed bid method is done by picking and filing the county bid form then you submit a day before the auction while the premium bid is made by auction until a high bid is reached. The premium includes interests, administrative costs, back taxes and penalty fees.

Arkansas

This is also a tax deed state; the sales are administered by the county and through the year. The starting bid here is the assessed value according to the state law, and the assessed value is usually 20% of the actual value of the property. The assessed value is then combined with the delinquent taxes of the next year. The real owner of the property before the sale has the right to redeem after the sale for up to 30 days. And if it so happens, the investor is refunded in full, the maximum tax delinquency years before foreclosure is two years in this state.

California

The early beginnings of spring months are used to carry out tax deed auction sales although the periods for the sales vary with different countries. The tax deed auctions are used to recover real property taxes. To participate in auctions, one has to complete his registration before the auction date, and in most cases, a minimum deposit is required from investors before they can bid.

The bidding site bid4assets.com conducts most of California's county tax deed auctions as it is mostly conducted online. Counties in this state also use the premium bid method which includes penalty fees, delinquent taxes, and administrative cost. The bidding continues until a higher bid is reached. The other two methods, sealed bid and agreement sale are not often used.

Connecticut

In the state of Connecticut, the sale is conducted by oral public auction, and the sales occur throughout the year as prescribed by the counties. The owner of the property has one year to redeem the property by paying the delinquent taxes and penalties or fees. Before the sale, the lists of properties to be auctioned are published in the local newspapers and magazines. When you win a bid and make all the necessary payments, a deed of the property will be issued to you by the tax collector and the deed stored for one year after which the redemption right is terminated if the owner does not make the necessary payments during that period.

The premium bid type is also used here. Back taxes, interest, and administrative are some of the charges placed upon the bid by the county.

Delaware

The county sheriff conducts the tax sales in 3 parts of this state. The initial bid price is determined by penalties, back taxes, interests, and costs. After a bid is won, the financial officer is sought to approve or disprove the sale made by the sheriff. The bid continues until a higher bid is reached using the premium bid method, with all the charges aforementioned.

The real owner of the property has 60 days to redeem from the time the sale was made, and if he so chooses to pay, the full amount of the bid and rate of return (15%) must be settled in full by him.

Florida

The state of Florida is a hybrid state. Each county holds tax lien and tax deed auctions. The counties conduct annual tax lien sales, and after a two-year period, the unsold tax liens are sold as tax deeds. The collector presides over the back taxes, penalty fees, and seizure of properties with unpaid taxes. The property auctions are advertised in the local newspapers before the sales date.

The redemption of tax lien certificates may be carried out within two years after April 1st of the year of the issuance of the tax certificate. When the two-year period expires, the county can issue a deed to the property. The county will hold a tax deed sale to determine the new property owner. Bidding will begin with the amount the certificate holder has invested in the property, plus the interest accrued. If the licence holder is outbid, or if he/she has no interest in gaining ownership of the property, the certificate holder will be reimbursed as if the original property owner had redeemed.

Idaho

This state also uses the tax deed to collect its delinquent property taxes. The period of which the tax collector can issue a deed on a property is three years. They also use the premium bidding in this state. But here, the board of county commissioners has the right to reject a sale after an auction is won, and they also determine the minimum bid based on the recommendation of the county treasurer. As with most of the states, the minimum bid consists of penalties, pending fees, delinquent taxes, publication cost, and interests.

Indiana

This is mostly classified as a tax lien state, but an investor can obtain a tax deed when he is holding a tax lien, and the owner of the property fails to pay the delinquent taxes, interests, and penalties at the end of a 12 month period. The tax sales are mostly conducted through the month of August to November, and the sales are public auction sales.

A lien holder is expected to begin a foreclosure process within nine months of the sale period, but the deed can only be obtained a year after the purchase and not later than six months after the expiration of the redemption period.

They also employ the premium bidding method here. The starting bid as always includes administrative cost, penalties, interests, and the back taxes. There is an excess fund referred to as 'tax sale overbid' which is the difference between the minimum bid and the successful bid price. It is kept as a tax sale surplus which may be given to the real owner of the property if he lost ownership or the lien certificate holder if the actual owner redeems the property.

Kansas

Arkansas is also a tax deed state, the month of August to October are used to carry out the tax sales. They as with other states of the US publish the list of properties to be auctioned 10 days before the sale. In some counties of Kansas, bidders are required to register early enough before the tax sale. The starting price is determined by the back taxes, interests accrued, penalties and administrative cost.

Counties in Kansas uses the premium bid method, and in some of them, bidding may even be started below the lien, and the highest bidder above the minimum bid goes with the property. In the case of tax deeds, the combined sum of the interests, penalties, and fees determine the starting bid price and the deeds are sold to the highest bidder also.

Michigan

In this state, the treasurer or tax collector is saddled with the responsibility of selling a property with delinquent taxes to the winning bid. The sales are carried out between the months of July to November every year. When unpaid taxes accrue on a property, the property is foreclosed within the month of March and April, and thus, it cannot be sold by the owner afterward. The counties of Houghton, Baraga, and Gogebic hold annually there in the month of August.

Maine.

Here, the tax collector is also responsible for the sale of delinquent property tax deeds at an auction and to the highest bidder. When you win and pay the requirements, the property becomes yours.

Minnesota

Likewise in Minnesota, the tax collectors or treasurers in the county sell off the delinquent property tax deeds at an auction to the highest bidder.

Nevada

So also In Nevada, the county tax collectors and treasurers sell tax deeds to the winning bid at the delinquent tax deed sales.

New Mexico

Unlike in many of the states where tax deed sales are handled by the county treasurers or tax collectors, in New Mexico, the sales are dealt with by the state itself. A period of three months is given of delinquency after which on non-payment of the back taxes, the property account is passed over to the state by the treasurer/tax collector.

The state then proceeds with the collection or foreclosure of the property. And as always, the property is sold to the highest bidder at an auction.

New York

New York City has five counties conjoined together as boroughs. They are Manhattan (New York County), Queens (Queens County), Brooklyn (Kings County), Bronx (Bronx County), Stanton Island (Richmond County). An investor can obtain information on a property from the government agencies, made possible by the freedom of information. Thus, maps, landmarks, and relevant property data can be obtained from the authority in charge of it free of charge.

At an auction deed, tax deeds are sold to the highest bidder by the treasurer or tax collector, and a property transfer report must accompany it.

North Carolina

And likewise In North Carolina, the tax collector or treasurer will sell the tax deeds to the winning bidders at the delinquent property tax sales.

Ohio

The state of Ohio sells both tax deeds and tax liens, many of the counties in this state, hold tax deed foreclosure auctions. Only counties with a high population sell tax lien certificates, the rest of the counties sells limited to tax deeds. The norm with starting bids in counties here is 2/3 of the property's actual value. The fiscal deeds of properties are sold to the bidder with the highest bid.

Oklahoma

This state also sells both tax liens and tax deeds. They offer about three types of sales, the tax sales, re-sales and county commissioner's sales. The re-sale is what is known commonly as the tax deed sale, and it occurs when a property with sold liens remain unredeemed for two years from the sales date. The sales auction takes place on the second Monday of the month of June.

Oregon

In the state of Oregon, the tax collector or treasurer is the one saddled with the responsibility of selling property tax deeds just as in some state counties. The bidder with the highest bid wins, and after paying the prescribed bills, the property becomes his. The state of Oregon offers finance to purchasers.

Pennsylvania

The tax claim bureau department handles the delinquent tax foreclosure properties within the counties of this state. The counties regularly hold two different tax sales, first the upset sale and secondly to remove tax liens.

The tax collector or treasurer sells the tax deeds to the winning bid at the delinquent property tax sale auction. The bidder willing to pay the most wins the bidding contest.

If in the two auctions a property remains, a repository list is created whereby a property can be purchased by mail offer, i.e. over the counter purchase. Some counties do even hold third auctions.

Tennessee

The state of Tennessee is a redeemable deed state. It is quite different than other deed states because when a bid is won, an investor must apply for a writ of possession and when approved he can collect rent on the property until it is redeemed. This to most investors is paid much. The redemption period is one year in Tennessee.

There is an interest rate of 10% added to a surplus overbid together with the full amount of the tax deed price. The opening bid includes the fees, administrative costs, penalties, and interests. The investor can only take full possession of the property one year after the bid is won.

Utah

The state of Utah conducts its tax deed sales on the same day and starts at the same time across the counties. When you choose the county you want to bid in, it is best you check the entire requirement from the local tax authority or look up in the local newspapers for any information prior to the sales day.

You can as well hire someone to represent you in other counties, the counties require immediate payment of any bid won. And it takes about 30 days for you to get the tax deed from the county when you win and make the necessary payments.

The mode of payment in this state is mostly cash or cashier's check. There is an opportunity for an investor to purchase a property at the opening bid price if the property didn't sell at the tax deed sale auction. This can be done by contacting the county's tax collection authority.

A property with delinquent taxes has a period of 5 years to be paid before it can sell by the county. If the owner wishes to pay the taxes and fees incurred, he has up to the period before the auction starts after which the property cannot be redeemed. They frequently advertise the auction sales on the local newspaper four weeks in advancement, and the auction does take place at the county courthouse.

Washington

Washington is a hybrid state in some ways because first, the county authorities hold tax lien certificates of delinquent tax properties for 3 years. If the owner still refuses to pay the taxes and charges within that three years period, a deed auction is held. But before that, they will publish a list of tax deed properties in the local papers three weeks before the auction date, and the owner has up until 5:00 pm the day before the sales day to pay and have his property removed from the auctions.

An investor or a bidder is required by the authorities to register before the auction day, or before the bidding starts on the same day, you can even send a representative to bid in your honor, but the appropriate authority should be notified before the bidding starts. The bidding amount takes into cognizance the administrative costs; the interests accrued, the penalties and the back taxes. They also use the oral, premium bid method in Washington. The bid continues until a higher bidder is found starting with the minimum bid price set for the property.

Wisconsin

The state of Wisconsin offer tax lien certificate on all properties with delinquent taxes in the month of September every year; this is solely the responsibility of each county's treasurer. The county then keeps the lien for two years, a period is given for the real owner to pay off the interest, penalties and back taxes to redeem his property. Afterward i.e. when the two year redemption period elapses by the 31st of August of the second year, the county treasurer forecloses the property, and a tax deed sale is initiated which is to be carried out by auction.

The deeds are to be sold and the property transferred to the highest bidder at the auction. The list of properties to be sold is published in the local newspapers.

Some counties accept sealed bids in Wisconsin; this method is the way by which an investor picks and completes a proposal form together with the amount he is bidding for, then encloses and submits it to the county tax collection officer. They practice the premium bid for the auction sales.

Conclusion
Lastly, when investing, be sure you contact people already in the business and learn one or two things from them. Thanks for purchasing this book.

www.ingramcontent.com/pod-product-compliance
Lightning Source LLC
Chambersburg PA
CBHW021001180526
45163CB00006B/2451